D1446201

Young Entrepreneurs

Run Your Own

Babysitting

Business

Emma Carlson Berne

PowerKiDS press.

New York

Published in 2014 by The Rosen Publishing Group, Inc.
29 East 21st Street, New York, NY 10010

First Edition

Editor: Joanne Randolph
Book Design: Andrew Povolny
Photo Research: Katie Stryker

Photo Credits: Cover Soren Hald/Cultura/Getty Images; p. 4 Helga Esteb/Shutterstock.com; p. 5 Jeff Whyte/Shutterstock.com; p. 6 Christian Muller/Shutterstock.com; p. 7 Photo and Co/Lifesize/Thinkstock; pp. 8, 13, 14–15, 16, 20, 23, 30 iStockphoto/Thinkstock; p. 10 Aletia/Shutterstock.com; p. 11 Tetra Images/Getty Images; p. 12 Anneka/Shutterstock.com; p. 17 Vartanova Anatoly/Shutterstock.com; p. 19 Tim Hall/Cultura/Getty Images; p. 21 Boris Suntsov/Flickr/Getty Images; p. 24 Pressmaster/Shutterstock.com; pp. 25, 26 Poznyakov/Shutterstock.com; p. 28 Jaimie Dupless/Shutterstock.com; p. 29 JGI/Jamie Grill/Blend Images/Getty Images.

Library of Congress Cataloging-in-Publication Data

Berne, Emma Carlson.
  Run your own babysitting business / Emma Carlson Berne. — First edition.
     pages cm. — (Young entrepreneurs)
  Includes index.
  ISBN 978-1-4777-2922-9 (library binding) — ISBN 978-1-4777-3011-9 (pbk.) — ISBN 978-1-4777-3082-9 (6-pack)
  1. Babysitting—Juvenile literature. 2. Babysitters—Juvenile literature. 3. Money-making projects for children—Juvenile literature. I. Title.
  HQ769.5.B47 2014
  649'.10248—dc23
                                        2013034777

Manufactured in the United States of America

CPSIA Compliance Information: Batch #W14PK2: For Further Information contact Rosen Publishing, New York, New York at 1-800-237-9932

Contents

You Can Be an Entrepreneur

When you think of the word **"entrepreneur,"** maybe you picture a person in a suit, leading a meeting in a skyscraper. You probably wouldn't picture yourself, an ordinary kid. You can be an entrepreneur, too, though. If you are hardworking and organized and have a good idea, you can create and run your own business.

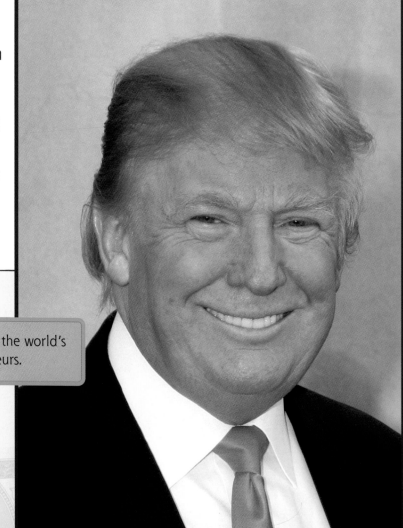

Donald Trump is one of the world's most famous entrepreneurs.

You do not have to own a multimillion-dollar corporation to be an entrepreneur. The owner of this food truck is an entrepreneur, too.

In this book, we'll discuss the steps you will need to follow, which include finding a need in your community, making a **business plan** that fulfills that need, creating a **budget**, opening and running the business and, of course, enjoying the **profits**!

Anyone Need a Babysitter?

Every business needs customers, and customers will only **patronize** a business that provides **goods** or **services** that they need. To get an idea of what sort of business you might like to start, look around at your community. What kinds of services are your parents or neighbors using? Is there a service people could use but that nobody else is providing? Can you provide one of these?

Walking your neighbors' dogs is one business idea. If most of your neighbors do not own dogs, though, you might want to keep brainstorming for new ideas.

If there are lots of kids in your neighborhood or apartment building, and you enjoy taking care of younger children, then babysitting could be the right business for you.

Babysitting can be a great business for a young person. Most likely, your neighborhood has plenty of children and babies. Parents sometimes need a break or need to run errands without their children. You can provide a service for which there is a built-in need.

Have a Plan

Now that you know you're going to run a babysitting service, you'll want to write down your business plan. This plan will outline where, when, and how you will run your business.

For a babysitter, the "where" of your business is easy. Most likely, you'll babysit in your **clients'** homes. You will be a traveling business.

It is a good idea to keep a notebook with you wherever you go. This way, you can jot down any new ideas or thoughts you have about your business.

The "when" is a little trickier than the "where." Are you going to babysit only on weekends? Will you take jobs after school? Are you permitted to babysit in the evenings? Is this strictly a summer business or will you work during the school year? When you create your business plan, you will want to sit down with your parents and discuss your boundaries.

Tip Central

Consider creating a **contract** with your parents about when you are allowed to babysit. Ask them to sign it and then sign it yourself. That way, everyone involved is clear on the rules.

Smartphones or computers can be great tools to keep you organized, too.

Though you may not always want to admit it, parents can be a good source of information. Tell them your plan. They might notice something you've missed.

Then focus on the "how." How are you going to get your business going? You can't do any babysitting until you have a good **reputation** as a caregiver. Parents will want to know that you are responsible, fun, and reliable. To spread your reputation, ask people for whom you've already babysat to tell their friends that you are a good sitter.

Building a Budget

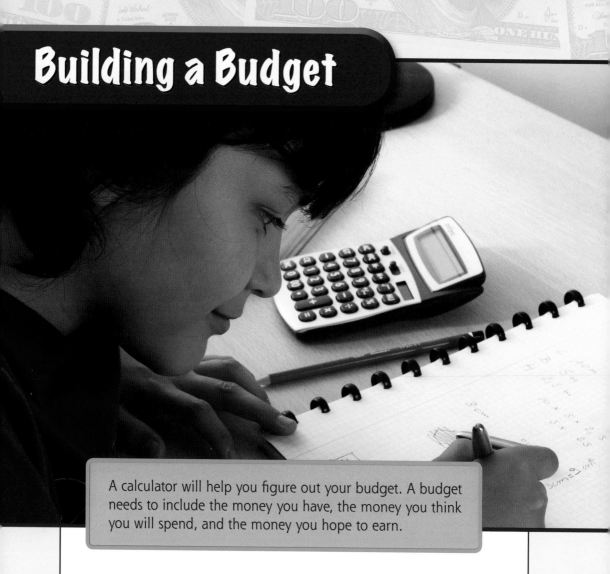

A calculator will help you figure out your budget. A budget needs to include the money you have, the money you think you will spend, and the money you hope to earn.

All good business owners know that to make money, you have to spend money. The money you spend is called your **expenses**. As a successful entrepreneur, you will want to minimize your expenses in order to maximize your profits.

You need to budget for your advertising supplies, such as paper, markers, and craft supplies. You also need to budget for a calculator that will help you create the rest of the budget!

To know how much money you should expect to spend, you will want to create a budget for your babysitting business. Write down everything you might need to spend money on. Maybe you will need supplies for crafts and books to take to jobs, materials to make advertising signs, and perhaps money to pay a parent for the gas it takes to drive you to far-away jobs. Look up how much each item will cost, write it down, and circle the total.

After you've written down your potential expenses, consider how much money you already have saved. If you don't have enough, you'll need to go into **debt** and borrow some. You will probably have to borrow from your parents. Write down exactly how much you borrowed and when you plan to pay it back. Then sign this contract and give it to your parents. This will make them feel that you have real plans to pay them back.

To start your budget, you first want to figure out how much money you already have that you can invest, or put into, your business.

Expenses	
Advertising Supplies	$15.00
Board Games/Craft Supplies	$25.00
Total	**$40.00**

Capital	
Savings	$35.00
Allowance	$5.00
Total	**$40.00**

Expenses – Capital = Total to Borrow

$40.00 – $40.00 = $0.00

You will want to include in your budget the amount of savings you are willing to put toward your business. Subtract your costs and you will see whether you have enough to start your business or whether you need a loan.

Tip Central

Build a little extra money into your budget as a cushion. Often, an unexpected expense will arise. You'll want to have enough money to cover it.

Advertise Your Services

All good babysitters need one very important thing. They need kids to babysit! In order to attract customers, you will need to advertise. Advertising will do two things. It will let the parents in your neighborhood know the basics about you: your name, how old you are, and the ages of kids you're interested in sitting for.

You can make posters with markers or paint, or you can make them on the computer and print them out. If you make them by hand, be sure to write neatly so customers can easily read your signs.

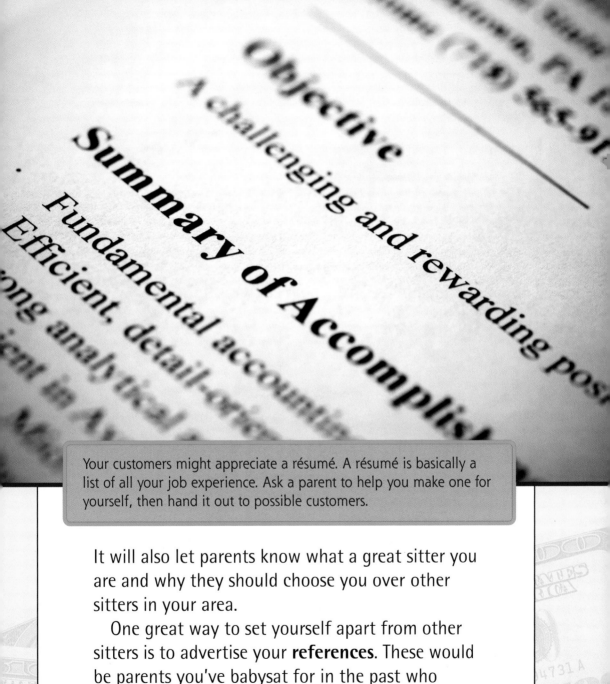

Your customers might appreciate a résumé. A résumé is basically a list of all your job experience. Ask a parent to help you make one for yourself, then hand it out to possible customers.

It will also let parents know what a great sitter you are and why they should choose you over other sitters in your area.

One great way to set yourself apart from other sitters is to advertise your **references**. These would be parents you've babysat for in the past who can **vouch** for your skills. "Excellent references available!" you might advertise.

Consider what advertising options are in your budget. Can you hang up signs at local preschools or day care centers? Be sure to check with the person in charge as some of these places have rules about who can post signs. How about the library or a café in your neighborhood? Do any of these places have bulletin boards for ads? Try to think of places where moms and dads with young children are likely to go. These are good places to post your signs.

Tip Central

Word of mouth can be excellent advertising for your business. Ask your parents and friends to tell other people that you are available as a babysitter and how to reach you.

If you hang signs on community message boards, make sure your poster stands out. There is a lot to look at on a message board and you don't want people to miss your sign.

Organization Counts

2

9

10
4 PM SMITHS

11

12

18

19

17

16
7 PM
COSTELLOS

25

24

23

When you take a job, be sure to write it down on your calendar. Your clients are counting on you, so you do not want to forget. Be sure to arrive a few minutes ahead of time, too.

Once you start advertising, you'll want to have a plan already in place for how to organize your clients. Decide ahead of time how much you will charge per hour. You can ask your friends who babysit how much they charge. Then, if you want, you could charge the same or maybe even slightly less, to undercut your competition.

When your clients call, greet them in a friendly way, let them know how much you charge, then write the appointment down in a planner or on a calendar. That way, you can keep track of exactly how many jobs you have each week.

Come prepared with modeling clay, some books, or board games to play with the children for whom you are babysitting.

Once you've scheduled a job, ask your clients a series of prewritten questions so you can get some details about their children. You might want to ask them about their basic expectations for the time you'll be babysitting, the children's likes and dislikes, favorite activities, and any specific fears. If you will be feeding the children a meal, ask about food allergies and what foods the children like. Find out about bedtime routines and timing, too, if you will be putting the children to bed. Take notes so you can look back at them on the day of the job.

Tip Central

If your client has more children than you are comfortable watching alone, ask if you can bring a friend to help. Be sure to offer your friend's full name, phone number, and his references. Also, let your client know the difference in price for two babysitters as opposed to one.

Most kids love to play. Think of some games you can play, such as soccer or freeze tag, and then suggest them to the children you are watching.

Get Creative

Most of your clients will want you to watch their children in their own homes. A good entrepreneur, though, should also think about creative ways to expand her business. Consider other ways you can provide child care in your community. Do you have a local arts center that has classes for kids?

During parent-teacher conference week, many parents often need a sitter for just a short time. You can charge a small amount per child, knowing you will likely still make a lot of money.

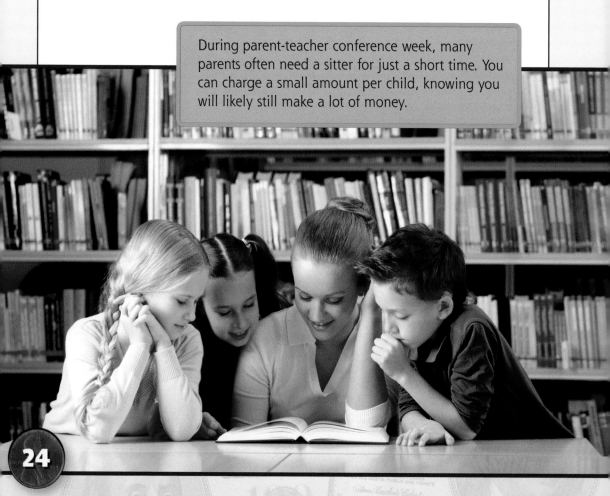

Advertise that parents can drop their kids off for 2 hours of bowling and what you will charge. Be sure to charge enough to cover the cost of the bowling and shoe rental. If you think you will have lots of kids, ask a friend to help you.

Maybe you can offer a Parents' Night Out there, and use that space. You can ask three or four friends to help you, and charge a flat fee for the hours of six o'clock to eight o'clock, for instance. Then you and the other babysitters can split the money.

Tip Central

Keep the ratio of kids to babysitters low during group sessions. Try to have no more than three kids for each babysitter.

Parents always appreciate having sitters when school is out for the day. They also need help with the kids for certain events, such as during parent-teacher conferences. Why not offer a Conference Special? Parents can drop kids off in the school library when they come in for their conference. You can entertain the children with quiet activities and stories. You can even print up special posters just for this event, and post them around the school. Of course, you'll want to get permission from the school principal and librarian first.

Plan fun activities for your group babysitting job. You can offer face painting, dancing, games, and other fun things to do.

Getting Down to Business

Congratulations! You've planned your business well, and now you're going out to babysit regularly. Watching kids isn't your only job, though. Keep careful track of any purchases you make over time, such as craft supplies. Also be sure to record all the money you have coming in. Each month, compare how much you are spending with how much money you're making.

You want to be sure the kids you babysit have fun so they want you to come back.

When a client pays you for a job well done, say thank you, then ask if she will be a reference or pass on your information to her friends.

Keep thinking of ways to expand, too. Ask your current clients to refer you to a friend, and offer them a discount on their next babysitting session if they do. Soon, you'll have a large, stable business and plenty of profits!

Are You Ready?

On a separate sheet of paper, check off these items to make sure you have everything ready for your babysitting business.

☐ Create a list of babysitting supplies, including a calendar for appointments, business cards, paper and markers for flyers, craft supplies like Popsicle sticks, pipe cleaners, glue, glitter, ribbon, puzzles, coloring books, and storybooks.

☐ Create a budget, including the money needed to open your business. Borrow money if necessary.

☐ Shop for supplies.

☐ Draw advertising flyers.

☐ Hold a meeting with your parents about babysitting rules and schedule.

☐ Distribute flyers and business cards around town.

☐ Record jobs on your calendar as they come in.

☐ Go out to babysitting jobs and have fun!

☐ Track your profits and enjoy your spending money!

Babysitting can be a fun and rewarding job. You must be responsible and flexible, though. Is babysitting the right business for you?

Glossary

budget (BUH-jit) A plan to spend a certain amount of money in a period of time.

business plan (BIZ-nes PLAN) Something that lays out who will run a business, what it will sell, when and where it will sell it, and how it will be set up and run.

clients (KLY-ents) People who pay a company or other people to do something.

contract (KAHN-trakt) An official agreement between two or more people.

debt (DET) Something owed.

entrepreneur (on-truh-pruh-NUR) A businessperson who has started his or her own business.

expenses (ik-SPENTS-ez) Costs.

goods (GUDZ) Products sold to others.

patronize (PAY-truh-nyz) To be a customer or client of a business.

profits (PRAH-fits) The money a company makes after all its bills are paid.

references (REH-frens-ez) People who will tell others about work you have done.

reputation (reh-pyoo-TAY-shun) The ideas people have about another person, an animal, or an object.

services (SIR-vis-ez) Things that a person does for other people.

vouch (VOWCH) To guarantee that someone has certain skills or credibility.

word of mouth (WURD UV MOWTH) People talking to one another, especially about a business or service.

Index

B

budget, 5, 13, 18
business plan, 5,
    8, 10

C

community,
    5–6, 24
contract, 14
customers, 6, 16

D

debt, 14

E

expense(s), 12, 14

G

goods, 6

H

homes, 8, 24

P

parent(s), 6–7,
    10–11, 13–14,
    16–17, 27, 30

profits, 5, 12,
    29–30

R

references, 17
reputation, 11

S

service(s), 6–8
supplies, 13,
    28, 30

Websites

Due to the changing nature of Internet links, PowerKids Press has developed an online list of websites related to the subject of this book. This site is updated regularly. Please use this link to access the list:
www.powerkidslinks.com/ye/sitter/